D0442972

DATE DUE			

Magic Johnson

By
Michael E. Goodman

CRESTWOOD HOUSE

New York

#30633

Goodman, Michael E.
  Magic Johnson

(SCU-2)
  1. Johnson, Earvin, 1959 — Juvenile literature. 2. Basketball players — United States — Biography — Juvenile literature. 3. Los Angeles Lakers (Basketball team) — Juvenile literature. I. Title. II. Series.
GV884.J63G66   1988   796.32'3'0924—dc19   88-20982
ISBN 0-89686-382-4

International Standard Book Number:	Library of Congress Catalog Card Number:
0-89686-382-4	88-20982

PHOTO CREDITS

Cover: Focus West: Joel Zwink
Focus West: 12, 26, 30-31, 45; (Rick Stewart) 4, 38, 42; (Jonathan Daniel) 7;
   (Robert Beck) 22, 34; (Stephen Dunn) 28, 33, 41; (Scott Cunningham) 36-37
Wide World Photos, Inc.: 9, 14, 16, 19, 21, 25

—for my friend Andy, a dedicated Magic Johnson and Laker fan—

Copyright © 1988 by Crestwood House, Macmillan Publishing Company

All rights reserved. No part of this book may be reproduced or transmitted in any form or by any means, electronic or mechanical, including photocopying, recording, or by any information storage and retrieval system, without permission in writing from the Publisher.

Macmillan Publishing Company
866 Third Avenue
New York, NY 10022
Collier Macmillan Canada, Inc.

Printed in the United States of America
10   9   8   7   6   5   4   3

TABLE
OF
CONTENTS

A MAGIC HOOK SHOT

Just four seconds were left in game 4 of the 1987 National Basketball Association championship series. The scoreboard above Boston Garden read: Boston 106, Los Angeles 105. The Boston fans were nervous and excited. If their Celtics could hold on for four more seconds, they would tie the Los Angeles Lakers in the battle for the 1987 NBA title. Each team would have won two games and lost two games. But the Lakers had "magic" on their side — the best player in basketball that year, Earvin "Magic" Johnson.

Magic received the inbounds pass from a teammate. He looked to pass underneath the basket, but Laker star Kareem Abdul-Jabbar was covered. He wanted to take a jump shot, but three Celtic players leaped out at him. He knew he didn't have enough time to duck under the defenders and shoot a jump shot. So Magic moved quickly toward the foul line with the ball. With his back to the basket, he lofted a hook shot toward the goal. It swished right through, magically! Los Angeles had won, they had a commanding three-games-to-one lead in the championship series. The Lakers were soon going to be champs again — for the fourth time in the eight years since Magic Johnson had joined the team.

Magic always smiles when he plays basketball. Earvin Johnson's two trademarks are his bright smile and his exciting style on the basketball court. After the game, Magic had a bigger smile than usual on his face!

Although he's taller than any other NBA point guard, Magic Johnson is smooth and quick.

MAGIC DOESN'T FIT THE USUAL PATTERN

Magic Johnson doesn't fit any of the usual patterns of a professional basketball player. Magic plays point guard for the Lakers. That means that he's the player who handles the basketball most of the time. He passes it off to his teammates so that they can score. A point guard has to be a quick thinker and a great dribbler and passer. On most teams, the point guard is one of the smallest players on the team. Smaller players can usually move faster on the court. They can control the ball better than taller players because they don't have to dribble the ball as high.

But Magic is 6'9"—taller than any other point guard in the NBA, and yet he's just as smooth and quick. His height helps him see over the player who is guarding him. He can spot any teammates who are open for a shot. Magic's height also helps him get a rebound and then lead his team down court for a quick basket. Los Angeles coach Pat Riley says that since Magic joined the Lakers, every other coach has been trying to develop a 6'9" point guard—"but there's still only one."

Here is another way Magic is different. Most professional basketball players think about scoring as many points as they can. But not Magic. He is a very unselfish player. He learned back when he was in high school that it can be just as much fun to make a great pass so that a teammate can score as to make a great shot of his own.

Magic Johnson's greatest trick is not how well he plays

Magic Johnson knows what his job is—and he does it well!

himself, but how he makes everyone else on his team play better. His teammates know that when they are in position for a shot, Magic will find a way to get the ball to them. It is no surprise that the Lakers changed from a good team to a great team once Magic took control.

Most professional basketball players also find it difficult to get "up" for every game. It's hard to get excited for every basketball game every single night. Players travel thousands of miles, and live on the road for long periods at a time. But Magic brings his smile and his talent to every game. His biggest rival, Larry Bird of the Celtics, once said, "Magic is the only player I would pay money to see." Lots of people do pay to see Magic play…and he always gives them their money's worth.

Magic's combination of talent, height, unselfishness, and passing ability have made him a "triple threat." He can score lots of points, rack up assists (passes that lead to teammates' scores), and pull down many rebounds. In fact, Magic's ability in all three areas has led the NBA to create a new statistic, the "triple double." A player records a triple double if he gets ten or more points, assists, *and* rebounds in the same game. Magic is the master of the triple double. After all, the statistic *was* created because of him!

EARNING HIS NICKNAME

Earvin Johnson Jr. was born in Lansing, Michigan, on August 14, 1959. He was the sixth of ten children. The

Magic poses with his parents after being drafted by the Los Angeles Lakers in 1979.

Johnson family was not rich, but the family was strong in love and respect for each other. Magic's father, Earvin Sr., worked two full-time jobs as an auto factory worker and a trash collector to support the large family. His mother had a full-time job as a junior high school cafeteria worker.

All of the Johnsons, adults and children, were involved in church activities. Magic particularly enjoyed taking part in the church choir. His mother thought he might be a singer or musician in the future. But Magic had one great love—

basketball. He played all of the time. When he couldn't get to a basketball court, he would roll up socks in his bedroom and shoot them toward an imaginary basket. Instead of cheers, however, he got scoldings from his mother. She didn't appreciate the noise or destruction that occurred when young Earvin or his brothers crashed into the furniture.

By the time Earvin was in the seventh grade, he was already six feet tall. He grew four more inches by eighth grade, and another inch by ninth grade. His skill and his reputation were also growing. All of the best players in Lansing, even high schoolers, came to the west side of town to take on Earvin Johnson.

Besides his parents, other people helped Earvin during these early school years. Two people who took an interest in him were Jim and Greta Dart. Mrs. Dart had been his fifth grade teacher. Mr. Dart volunteered to supervise Earvin and other kids so that they could practice in the school gym after hours. The Darts helped Earvin find part-time jobs to help out his family, and they sent him to a summer basketball camp.

Earvin also turned to Dr. Charles Tucker, a psychologist in the Lansing schools, for advice. Dr. Tucker had been a fine college basketball player and had once tried out for a pro team. Earvin met Dr. Tucker at his school, and they began to play one-on-one basketball games together. Soon they became close friends. They are still close friends today.

One of Earvin's first decisions was whether or not to play basketball for Everett High School. The coach there was George Fox. He had once cut Earvin's brother Larry from his team, and Earvin wasn't sure he wanted to play for Coach

Fox's team. Earvin talked over the problem with Dr. Tucker and then decided to show Coach Fox that the Johnsons were good players.

When he was a sophomore, Earvin became a starter at Everett. At first, Coach Fox wanted to make him play according to set patterns. But Earvin liked to create shots and plays as he went along. He was so good at being creative, and the team was winning so often, that Coach Fox decided to let Earvin play his own kind of game. Earvin jumped center on the team. He also brought the ball up court, and then played near the basket as a forward. In other words, he did it all.

In one game, Earvin scored 36 points, had 18 rebounds, 14 assists, and 5 steals. What do you call a player who can do all that? One Lansing sportswriter had the answer. He decided to give the young star a nickname. It couldn't be the "Big E." That name belonged to NBA star Elvin Hayes. It couldn't be "Dr. J." Julius Erving already owned that one. "How about 'Magic'?" the writer suggested. Perfect! From that day on, Earvin Johnson Jr. became Magic Johnson.

Magic led Everett High School to a 22-2 record during his sophomore year. Not bad for a team that had been 11-12 the year before Magic arrived! The team's second loss came in the quarterfinals of the state tournament. Magic was upset not only because his team lost but also because he had missed several important foul shots near the end of the game.

Magic received a big honor for his play during the year — he was named to the Michigan All State high school basketball team. He wasn't satisfied, however, because his team hadn't won a big honor, too. He was determined to do better the next year.

AN UNSELFISH STAR

Everett High lost only three games in the next two years. One of those losses came in the state semifinals in Magic's junior year. Magic earned All State honors again that year,

but he still wasn't satisfied.

Then came Magic's senior year. He was unstoppable in the first three games, scoring 54 points in one game and averaging 45 points for the three contests. But the team wasn't clicking. The fans focused all of their attention on Magic, and so did his teammates. All of the other Everett players stood around while Magic dribbled the ball and shot it.

Coach Fox had a talk with his star. Together they decided that Magic should change his style for the good of the team. Magic didn't really mind. He got a big thrill out of making a great pass and earning an assist while a teammate made a basket. He was still in control of the game, and his creativity was being put to the test on nearly every play.

By the end of the year, Magic's scoring average had dropped to just under 24 points per game. And Everett High was the 1976 Michigan state basketball champion!

Magic was named to the All State team for the third straight year. College coaches were lined up to try to convince Earvin to bring his "magic" to their schools. He had another big decision to make.

Magic has had one great love all his life—basketball.

Magic (No. 33) played college basketball for the Michigan State Spartans.

THE GREEN AND WHITE

After much thought, Magic narrowed down his decision to two colleges—the University of Michigan and Michigan State University. It was a hard choice. Michigan usually had one of the better teams in the Big Ten Conference, while Michigan State had not won the league championship in nearly 20 years. Magic liked the idea of playing for a winner, but he figured he could help State become a winner, too. State was also in East Lansing, just a few miles from his home. His family and friends would be able to see him play there. Besides, his father was already a big MSU fan. So Magic decided to wear the green and white uniform of the Michigan State Spartans. Magic predicted that his new team was not only going to be a winner, but the NCAA champion, too. It took only two years for him to help make this prediction come true.

The Spartan fans were ready to support a winner. They even began packing the school gym for team practices. Finally, the crowds got so big that Coach Jud Heathcote had to close his practices to the fans. He wanted his players to concentrate on the drills and plays they needed to learn.

Magic worked hard on his outside shooting, the one weakness in his game. And he perfected his "no look" passes. NBA and Laker fans are familiar with those. Magic moves across the court at top speed. He doesn't seem to notice his teammates who are running or standing near him. The defender thinks Magic is going to shoot the ball himself, but at the last second he passes it off to a teammate on either side of him—without looking. The unguarded teammate makes a basket. Two points for Magic's team!

All of the hard practice paid off. By the end of the season, the Spartans had won 25 games and lost only 5. No other Michigan State team had ever won more than 20 games. The team had also won the Big Ten championship for the first time in 19 years. Now they were off to the NCAA basketball tournament. The winner of that tournament would wear the

Several pro basketball teams noticed young Magic Johnson (far left) as soon as he began playing college ball.

crown as the best team in college basketball. Would Magic's prediction of a Michigan State championship come true?

The Spartans won their first two games in the tournament. Then they met the powerful Kentucky Wildcats in the Mideast Regional Finals. Kentucky had been rated the top team in the country all year long. MSU just wasn't strong enough to beat Kentucky. The Wildcats held Magic in check and won the game. Ten days later, Kentucky won the national championship.

Magic was disappointed that the Spartans had lost, but he was happy with how well the team had played. Many sportswriters and coaches were happy with the way Magic had played, too. They voted him to the All Big Ten Team, and he was the only freshman in the country named to an All American team.

Magic enjoyed all of the honors, but he suddenly had another big decision to make. Several pro basketball teams wanted Magic to play for them. One team offered him a contract for $250,000 a year for six years. With all of that money, Magic could help his family, and his parents wouldn't have to work as hard. He thought about the money and about playing pro basketball against the best players in the world. He also thought about his prediction that Michigan State would win the NCAA crown. And he thought about continuing his college education. After all, he would need his college degree when he finished playing basketball. His parents really wanted him to stay in school, too. Their wishes mattered the most to Magic. He decided to return to MSU for his sophomore year.

THE COLLEGE CROWN

Everyone expected Michigan State to be the top team in the Big Ten during the 1978-1979 season. But things didn't start out so well. The Spartans had a slump in the middle of the season and lost four of their first eight Big Ten games. Some writers said Magic wasn't doing his job. It was the first time Magic had ever been criticized in the newspapers, and he didn't like it. The team called a meeting with Coach Heathcote and talked over what they needed to do to be a winner. The talk worked! The Spartans won nine of their last ten games and finished the season tied for first in their league. They were rated as one of the top six teams in the country.

The best team in the country that year was Indiana State. The Sycamores were led by a spectacular 6'9" shooter named Larry Bird. Many people considered Bird and Magic the two best college players, and they wondered if they would meet in the NCAA tournament.

At first, things didn't look so good for Michigan State. Magic's friend and teammate Jay Vincent hurt his leg in the first tournament game against Lamar. That meant that Magic and the others would have to play harder. They did. The Spartans roared past Lamar, Louisiana State University, and Notre Dame to earn a spot in the Final Four. Indiana State also made the Final Four, along with number-two-ranked DePaul and the University of Pennsylvania.

MSU crushed Penn by 34 points to make it to the finals. The Spartans' big weapon was the "alley-oop" play in which Magic would lob the ball above the basket, sometimes

In college, Magic perfected his now-famous "alley-oop" play.

18

without looking. Greg Kelser would catch the ball above the rim and stuff it through the hoop. Along with his assists, Magic made nine out of the ten shots he took. He finished the game with 29 points.

Meanwhile, Indiana State downed DePaul in the other semifinal contest. The fans would have their wish. It would be Magic vs. Bird for the championship.

The game turned out to be no contest. Bird had a bad shooting game—one of the few in his career—and his teammates couldn't stop Magic or Michigan State's alley-oop play. Magic scored 24 points, grabbed 7 rebounds, and handed out 5 assists. Magic was the tournament's Most Valuable Player, and the Spartans were champs!

Once again, the pros began making offers to Magic. This time he listened more carefully. The Los Angeles Lakers would have the first pick in the upcoming college draft. Magic thought about playing on the same team with Kareem Abdul-Jabbar, the greatest scorer in basketball history. The Lakers were also offering him more than a half million dollars a year!

Magic talked over his decision with his parents and with Dr. Tucker. He promised his mother that he would continue to take courses when the pro basketball season was over and would eventually get his degree. Los Angeles would also be a great place for him to learn more about his field of study—communications. After all, Los Angeles and nearby Hollywood are where most television shows and movies are made. So Magic began packing his bags. Hollywood was going to have a new star.

Indiana State could not stop Magic and the Michigan State Spartans from winning the 1979 NCAA championship.

MAKING ADJUSTMENTS

Before Magic joined the Lakers, they were an above average team of steady but unexciting players. Fans who came to the Los Angeles Forum to watch the team play were pretty calm and quiet, too. In fact, some fans even took naps during a Laker game! That all changed when Magic came to town. He brought his smile and his style with him.

Even before the season began, it was clear that things were going to be different. Many of the Lakers' rookies played on a team in the Southern California Rookie League. Only about 400-to-500 fans usually turned out for these rookie games. But nearly 5,000 people came to watch Magic's first rookie game!

Magic was a great player, but he had a lot to learn in order to succeed in the pros. The first thing he had to learn was how to play as a team member with the other Lakers. Magic spent most of the time during pre-season practices studying his new teammates. He wanted to learn where and how they usually moved on the court, and what kind of passes they liked best. After all, he was going to be the one throwing most of those passes.

The first few practices were a little rocky. Many of Magic's "no look" passes went out of bounds because his teammates weren't looking for them either. He and the Lakers' other starting guard, Norm Nixon, also bumped into each other on the court many times. Nixon had been the point guard the year before. Both men wanted to run the team. They had to learn to share the job of handling the ball without getting in

The "no look" passes have fooled many opponents.

each other's way.

The Lakers won their first game of the season, 103-102, on a last second skyhook by Kareem Abdul-Jabbar. Papers around the country the next day showed the old veteran being hugged by a brightly smiling 19-year-old rookie — Magic. The old and the new were about to blend together into a winning combination. Magic called Kareem, "Big Fella," and Kareem called Magic, "Buck," because he had the energetic nature of a young bucking horse.

The Lakers had been expected to come in second to the Seattle Supersonics in the Pacific Division of the NBA in 1979-1980. The Supersonics had been NBA champs the year before. But Magic wasn't used to being number two. Magic, Kareem, Norm Nixon, and their teammates Jamaal Wilkes, Adrian Dantley, Jim Chones, and Spencer Haywood rolled past Seattle and the other Pacific teams to win the division title. The Lakers also won the most games of any team in the NBA that year. They were heading to the play-offs as a favorite to win the championship.

For Magic personally, it had also been a wonderful season. He averaged 18 points and 7.3 assists per game. He also grabbed 7.7 rebounds a game, the second highest average ever by an NBA guard. He was the first rookie to start on the All Star team in 11 years.

Magic was second in the voting for Rookie of the Year, however. Guess who won the award in 1980? Magic's college rival Larry Bird, who was now playing with the Boston Celtics. Those two men seemed to always be on the top together.

After a successful rookie season with the Lakers, Magic started on the All Star team.

Bird may have won the rookie award, but Magic and the Lakers were going to win a much bigger trophy.

WORLD CHAMPS

The Lakers moved swiftly through the first two rounds in the play-offs against the Phoenix Suns and Seattle

Supersonics. They were now in the finals against the Philadelphia 76ers, led by Dr. J., Julius Erving. The 76ers had defeated Boston to win the Eastern title. The first team to win four games would be the world champs for 1980.

The two teams split a pair of games in Los Angeles and two more in Philly. Then they headed back to LA, tied 2-2. Kareem played brilliantly in game 5 to put the Lakers up in the series. However, during the game Kareem sprained his ankle. No one knew whether he would be able to play again in the series.

When the teams flew back to Philadelphia for game 6, Kareem stayed behind. Without Kareem, the Lakers were sure to lose. That's what everyone thought. Everyone but the Lakers and their rookie star, Magic Johnson. LA coach Paul Westhead decided to try a magic trick himself in the sixth game. He named Magic Johnson to be his starting center to replace Kareem. Magic had not played center since high school. Would he be able to adjust to the strange new position?

He did more than adjust; he starred. Magic played 47 of the 48 minutes. He scored 42 points, grabbed 15 rebounds, made 7 assists, had 3 steals, and blocked 1 shot. The Lakers behind Magic and Jamaal Wilkes turned a 60-60 halftime tie into a 123-107 romp. The Lakers were champs, and Magic was once again an MVP (Most Valuable Player).

In three years, Magic Johnson's teams had won the Michigan state high school championship, the NCAA crown, and the NBA title. His smile and his fame were brighter than ever.

With Magic Johnson playing center, the LA Lakers became the 1980 NBA title champions.

THE TITLE JINX

The Lakers had a special challenge for the 1980-1981 season. No team had won the NBA title two years in a row since 1969. The Lakers wanted to break that jinx. It was not going to be an easy task.

Early in the season, Magic banged into the Dallas center and hurt his knee. He kept playing however. The team was winning, and Magic was the number-one assist man in the league and one of the top scorers. But when he tried to make a fast turn during a game against Kansas City, the knee gave way. He would need an operation.

Magic was out of the line-up for over three months. The Lakers were still able to stay atop their division without Magic, but many of the players were confused and unhappy because Coach Westhead kept changing their assignments. Magic returned for the last 18 games of the season, and LA won 11 of them. The Lakers had finished second in their division behind Phoenix, but with Magic back they thought they were ready to defend their crown.

Their dream ended quickly. The Houston Rockets shocked the Lakers in the first round of the play-offs. LA won the first game in the best two-out-of-three series. But Houston won at home and then in Los Angeles to end the Lakers' season.

Laker players and fans were disappointed, but team owner Jerry Buss started planning right away for the future. The first step in his plans was to make sure that Magic Johnson would always be a Laker. So Buss signed his young star to an unbelievable contract. He added 25 years onto Magic's

It's hard to block Magic when he's determined to make a basket.

Magic proudly poses in front of his home.

existing contract—at $1 million a year! Magic could play as many years as he wanted in a Laker uniform. Then he could choose to become a member of the team's coaching or business staff.

Magic now knew that his family would never have any more worries about money. He could concentrate on only one thing—playing basketball.

Magic's concentration was broken, however, by changes

that Coach Westhead wanted to make in the early part of the 1981-1982 season. The coach wanted more set plays. That meant that Magic couldn't be as free and creative as he liked. Several players grumbled in private about the changes, but Magic spoke right up. When the coach wouldn't listen, Magic went to the boss, Jerry Buss.

In less than a day, Coach Westhead was gone and replaced by former Laker player Pat Riley (Riley is still the Laker coach today). LA fans were angry at Magic for getting the coach fired, and they booed him at the next Laker home game.

The boos turned to cheers quickly as the Lakers won 17 of their next 20 games on their way to another Pacific Division title. Magic, meanwhile, racked up lots of "triple-doubles" during the year. He became only the third player in NBA history to have more than 700 points, 700 assists, and 700 rebounds in the same season. The other two were basketball legends Oscar Robertson and Wilt Chamberlain.

LA swept through the first two rounds of the play-offs, winning all eight games they played against Phoenix and San Antonio. They then beat Philadelphia in the first game of the finals. No other NBA team had ever won nine play-off games in a row.

The 76ers took the next game to end LA's winning streak, but the Lakers won games 3 and 4 to take a big 3-1 lead in the series. Philly won game 5, but game 6 was all LA and Magic. Magic scored a "lucky 13" triple-double—13 points, 13 assists, and 13 rebounds. LA had won its second title in three years, and Magic had won his second tournament MVP trophy.

During the 81-82 season, Magic became the third player to have more than 700 points, assists, and rebounds in the same season.

PASSING UP, SCORING DOWN, WINNING UP

The Lakers were determined that 1982-1983 was the year they were finally going to win their second NBA title in a row. To help the team toward that goal, Magic began to concentrate more on his passing than his shooting—that is what he had done in his senior year in high school. Magic's scoring average dropped from 18.6 to 16.8 points per game, but his assist average skyrocketed to more than ten per game. He was clearly the best passer in the league. He continued to score clutch points and to pull in lots of rebounds. In 16 of the 79 games he played during the season, Magic recorded a "triple-double." He led LA to another Pacific Division crown.

Magic's great play and unselfishness earned him a special honor of his own. He was named for the first time to the All NBA team. That means that Magic was voted one of the five best players in the league!

The Lakers were ready for the play-offs. They breezed by Portland in the first round and edged by San Antonio in the second round to make it to the finals again. In the six-game San Antonio series, Magic averaged a "triple-double"—17.5 points, 10.5 rebounds, and 14 assists per game.

It would be the Lakers against the 76ers another time in the NBA finals, just as in Magic's rookie year. This time, the 76ers were more than ready. Philadelphia still had Dr. J. on the team, and they had added another big weapon—center Moses Malone. The 76ers outshot and outmuscled the Lakers.

Magic was voted one of the five best players in the league after the 82-83 season.

Magic's concentration throughout every game usually means a win for the LA Lakers.

They swept the series, four games to none. The Lakers had failed again to conquer the NBA title jinx and win two in a row.

Another one of Magic's no look passes fools his opponents—but Magic's teammates are ready.

MAGIC VS. BIRD

In the next three seasons, two teams and two players rose clearly to the top of the league, head and shoulders above all the others. The two teams were the Lakers and the Boston Celtics. The Lakers easily had the best record in the Western Conference of the NBA, and the Celtics dominated the Eastern Conference.

The two best players were those long-time rivals, Magic Johnson and Larry Bird. During each of the three years, Bird was named the NBA's Most Valuable Player. He was the best clutch scorer in the league. Whenever the Celtics needed a basket, Bird found a way to score it.

At the same time, Magic was becoming an even more amazing passer. In three seasons he averaged 13.1, 14.3, and 13.6 assists per game. People who had been following basketball for a long time said that Magic was the best point guard ever.

Both Magic and Bird were named to the All NBA team in the 1983-1984 season, and it was certain that their teams would meet for the NBA championship. They did. Both teams defeated their opponents in the first two rounds and moved on to the finals. It would be the first showdown between Magic and Bird since Michigan State played Indiana State for the NCAA title in 1979.

Since the Celtics had won more games than LA during the regular season, they had the home-court advantage. That meant that the first two games of the series would be played in Boston. Also, if the series went the full seven games before one team won four times, the last game would be in Boston. The last fact was important. Boston had never lost a seventh game on their home court in the team's history. Boston had also never lost a final round to the Lakers, and the teams had met for the title six times before in league history.

The Lakers got off to a quick start as Kareem led them to a 115-109 win in Boston. The Celtics came back two days later with an overtime victory to tie the series. In Los Angeles, Magic recorded a "triple-double" to key the Lakers' win in game 3. Bird took over in game 4. He scored 29 points and had 21 rebounds in a four-point Celtic win. The Celtics won game 5 in Boston, and the Lakers took game 6 in LA. One more game to go. The seventh game was a real battle. Boston didn't shoot well from the field, but they sank 25 more free throws than the Lakers. The Celtics beat the Lakers again for the championship.

Now the question became: Would Boston be able to win two in a row? To do so, the Celtics would have to get by Magic and the Lakers again. Both teams ended the following season on top of their divisions and won their conference play-off titles. They were in the finals again. And Boston once again had the home-court advantage. This time, it didn't matter. In game 7 in Boston Garden, the Lakers finally changed history. Magic had another "triple-double," and Kareem scored 29 to lead LA to the championship. It was the first time in eight tries that the Lakers had beaten the Celtics. And still no team had won two titles in a row since 1969.

It was also the Laker's fifth time in the finals and third championship since Magic had joined the team. He was the key member of the team, not only because of his points and assists, but also because of the spirit he brought to the team. The Lakers, with Magic directing them, had become one of the most exciting teams in basketball. Magic's smile seemed

By 1985 the Lakers had become one of the most exciting teams in basketball.

to spread to all of the other Laker players. They had fun playing the games and their fans had fun watching. No one took a nap anymore at the Los Angeles Forum. There was too much noise!

LA fans cheered hard for their team to win the NBA championship again in 1985-1986, but the jinx was still too strong. The Lakers faced the Houston Rockets in the second round of the play-offs. A last second miracle shot by Ralph Sampson sent Houston to the finals instead of Los Angeles. There the Rockets fell to Boston and Larry Bird.

MAGIC'S GREATEST YEAR

Magic had won many honors in his NBA career, but he had never been named the league's Most Valuable Player. His friend Larry Bird had already won that honor three times in a row. His teammate Kareem Abdul-Jabbar had won the award a record six times. But 1986-1987 was going to be a "magic" season for the Lakers and Earvin Johnson.

Early in the year, Coach Riley took Magic aside. They discussed the fact that Kareem was getting older, almost 40, and could not score as many points as in the past. Riley also said that the Lakers were going to need more points scored by the guards to beat bigger, tougher teams such as the Houston Rockets. Magic was going to have to shoot more and score more, Riley said. He was going to have to be selfish sometimes.

Magic was worried that Kareem might be upset by his

In the 86-87 season, Magic averaged nearly 24 points a game.

taking over the scoring, but the big man told him, "You've got to average over 20 points a game for us to win."

Magic responded with an amazing year. He averaged nearly 24 points per game to lead the Lakers in scoring for the first time. And he still handed out a team record 977 assists. His 12.2 assists per game were tops in the league.

With Magic leading the way, the Lakers had the best record in the NBA in 1986-1987. That meant they would finally have the home-court advantage if they faced the Celtics in the finals. Of course, the two teams did meet again. Boston was going for two titles in a row this time, and the Lakers were once again in their way.

Magic pumped in 29 points in game 1 in Los Angeles to lead the Lakers to an easy 126-113 win. The Lakers bombed the Celtics again in game 2, 141-122. Heading to Boston, LA was up two games to none.

The Celtics won game 3, despite 32 points by Magic. That set the stage for game 4, and Magic's great game-winning shot — the one you read about at the beginning of this book. In that game, Boston was leading by one point with 29 seconds to go. Magic dribbled near the foul line and spotted Kareem open under the basket. He threw a perfect pass, and the big man stuffed the ball to put LA up by one point. Then Larry Bird took the inbounds pass, dribbled up the court, and calmly sank a three-point shot with 12 seconds to go to put Boston up by two.

Magic found Kareem again, and he was fouled under the basket with seven seconds to go. Kareem sank the first foul shot but missed the second which would have tied the game.

Even at home on his day off, Magic finds time to practice.

Boston's Kevin McHale tried to grab the rebound, but it bounced off his hands and went out of bounds. Four seconds to go.

Magic took the pass, threw in his hook shot, and LA was ahead with only two seconds left in the game. Boston still had a slim chance. Bird took the pass, dribbled twice and threw up a good shot, but it bounced off the rim. The Lakers were up 3-1.

Boston won game 5 at home, and the two teams headed back to LA with the Lakers having to win only one of the last two games to be champs again

Game 6 was all Magic. He had 19 assists in the game and only turned the ball over three times. The Celtics were up 56-51 at half-time, but in the third quarter the Lakers destroyed

them. LA scored 30 points in the period to 12 for Boston. Magic scored 12 of those points and assisted on 8 others. He also had 4 rebounds. One sportswriter wrote, "Can the game be played any better than Magic played it in the third period Sunday?" The answer is probably "No."

The Lakers were champs again, and Magic was the play-off MVP for the third time. He topped off the great year by finally winning the league MVP award as well. He was on top of the basketball world.

PROMISING A WIN

In the locker room after the 1987 finals—and on national television—Laker coach Pat Riley made a promise. He guaranteed that LA would win the championship again in 1988. The pressure was now on the team and its leader, Magic Johnson, to keep that promise.

Nagging injuries slowed down Magic all season long. His shooting percentage fell below .500 for the first time in his career, and his scoring average dropped to just under 20 points per game. Other key players were also hurt for part of the season. Still the Lakers won. They finished the year with the best record in basketball and prepared to defend their crown. Was this finally going to be the year for a repeat champion?

The Lakers demolished San Antonio in the first round, then faced Utah. The big, strong Jazz extended the series the full seven games before LA won. Magic broke loose in the final contest with 24 points and lots of assists to power LA to the division finals against Dallas. The Mavericks were prepared for an upset victory, but LA prevailed once again in seven games.

In the East, youth overcame experience as the Detroit Pistons romped over the Boston Celtics to reach the finals against the Lakers. Basketball fans prepared for a classic series between the "old" champ and the young challenger. The series had particular meaning to Magic. He would be playing in an NBA final before his family and friends in Michigan for the first time, and he would be squaring off against his closest friend, Isiah Thomas of the Pistons.

The Pistons won three of the first five games. The Lakers had their backs to the wall. Now they had to win both games 6 and 7 in the Forum. They did—just barely. In game 6, Kareem sank two foul shots with 14 seconds left to give the Lakers a one-point win. Then in game 7, the Lakers blew a 17-point fourth quarter lead to slip by with a 108-105 win.

Coach Riley hugged Magic in the locker room after the game and thanked him for helping to keep the promise. It was the Lakers' fifth title since 1980, the year Magic Johnson came to town.

A STAR ON AND OFF THE COURT

Magic Johnson is one of the greatest players in basketball history on the court. But he is also a remarkable person off the court. He has made many television commercials and personal appearances at schools and youth clubs to try to convince young people not to take drugs. He works with the Special Olympics to help mentally retarded children. He founded a special "Active Reading" program in his hometown of Lansing, Michigan, to help students who have reading problems. He has organized charity basketball games to raise money for the United Negro College Fund and other groups. He is always willing to give both his time and his money to help others.

Earvin Johnson is always smiling, and he brings out smiles in everyone around him. That's his special "magic."

MAGIC JOHNSON'S PROFESSIONAL STATISTICS

Year	Games	Field Goals	FG%	Free Throws	FT%	Assists	Rebounds	Points	Scoring Average
79-80	77	503	.530	374	.810	563	596	1387	18.0
80-81	37	312	.532	171	.760	317	320	798	21.6
81-82	78	556	.537	329	.760	743	751	1447	18.6
82-83	79	511	.548	304	.800	829	683	1326	16.8
83-84	67	441	.565	290	.810	875	491	1178	17.6
84-85	77	504	.561	391	.843	968	476	1406	18.3
85-86	72	483	.526	378	.871	907	426	1354	18.8
86-87	80	683	.522	535	.848	977	504	1909	23.9
87-88	72	490	.490	417	.850	858	449	1408	19.6
Totals	639	4483	.534	3189	.816	7037	4696	12213	19.2

#30633